D1118660

DEERFIELD

An American Garden Through Four Seasons

Derek Fell

Pidcock Press

Preceding page: *The Valley Garden in spring, looking upstream towards a spillway and old springhouse.*

Above: *Colorful grouping of mature trees and shrubs, including azaleas, rhododendrons, Japanese cut-leaf maples, green ash and copper beech.*

4

CONTENTS

Published by Pidcock Press
Box 1
Gardenville, PA 18926 (USA)
(215) 794-8187

Copyright © Derek Fell 1986
ISBN 0-9616111-0-3
Library of Congress Catalog
No. 85-63743

Designed and produced by
Odyssey Productions Ltd

All rights reserved. No part of this
publication may be reproduced,
transmitted or stored in any form or by
any means, electronic or mechanical,
including photocopy, recording or any
information storage and retrieval
system, without prior permission from
the author.

Printed in Hong Kong

Acknowledgements

In addition to individuals specifically
mentioned in the text, thanks are due
to the following people who helped
make this book possible:
  Bill Klein, Director of the Morris
Arboretum, Philadelphia, and Robert
W. Meyer, Curator, for help in
identifying trees; Toni Anne Flanigan
and Mark W. Deeken, for their
gardening expertise at Deerfield; Anita
Gormley and Peggy Conklin, for
secretarial help; and Magnus Bartlett,
Hilary Binks and Joan Law for editorial,
design and production skills.

H. Thomas Hallowell, Jr.
Derek Fell

Distributed by International Specialized Book Services, 5602 N.E. Hassalo Street,
Portland, OR 97213 (USA), (503) 287-3093.

INTRODUCTION

By H. Thomas Hallowell, Jr.

Five Springs Garden — formerly an overgrown thicket of brambles and poison ivy — just weeks after completion.

I am told this book about Deerfield garden is a first of its kind. Though colorful works have been published on other beautiful gardens — such as Sissinghurst in Kent, England, and Winterthur in Delaware, U.S.A. — they are about gardens open to the public through an admission charge. Deerfield, by contrast, is a very *private* garden, a country estate that values its seclusion. The over-riding purpose of this book is to share with others the beauty, tranquility and pleasure of a private paradise at the peak of its perfection, through all four seasons. Also, to express a philosophy of gardening and garden design which I personally have found successful.

The inspiration for this work sprang from my association with Derek Fell, whom I first met when he came to Deerfield to photograph the gardens for *Architectural Digest* magazine. I was impressed by his work — both his lively writing and his artistic photography showed a sensitivity to gardens I had not seen expressed before. The resulting feature in the October, 1981 issue of *Architectural Digest* gave me so much satisfaction and pleasure that I was encouraged to continue to improve the gardens . . . and ultimately to work with Derek on this book.

Another important influence on the garden has been Albert F.W. Vick, Jr., owner of Vick's Wildgardens, a company that specializes in landscaping with wild plants. Al first started working with me on an azalea garden fifteen years ago. I would sketch out ideas on scraps of paper as suggestions for Al so he could then carry out the construction and planting. If ever we disagreed, he always had the tact to give in to my point of view; if this proved wrong and we ended up doing it his way after all, he accepted the changes with good grace. That may sound terribly autocratic, but he has been a super person to work with and Deerfield has benefited from his experience. Nevertheless, all the most successful gardens I've seen were largely the responsibility of one person — usually the owner — and I never knew of a good one that resulted from the decisions of a committee.

In composing garden areas, I have found my interest in photography invaluable. For Christmas, 1934 my wife, Dorothy, gave me a fine camera and I've been a keen amateur photographer ever since. The best photographs require good composition, and with gardens the same is true. I am constantly looking at my garden as if I were looking through a camera viewfinder, arranging plants and structures so the scene makes a good composition for a photograph. Even after an area is planted, I never stop wondering how it can be changed to make a better photograph. When it photographs well, a garden planting generally looks good to the naked eye, too, though the reverse is not always the case.

Because of my desire to see my garden produce visually exciting photographs, I have always been fond of creating "vistas," and whenever a visitor to Deerfield comments on these, I know he has a good sense of garden appreciation. In gardens, as in day-to-day life, too many people are "close-up"-oriented and neglect the overall view. Flowers, shrubs and trees to me exist for one reason — to be the component parts of a pretty picture.

When something obstructs a beautiful view, I almost always have it removed. So often the quickest and most economical way to improve a landscape is with a saw for removing an offensive limb or even an entire tree. In 1964, when an adjacent property of fifteen acres with a Tudor-style mansion was offered for sale, I bought it to enlarge the Deerfield estate to fifty acres. However, I had no real use for the house with its quarters for six servants, and it spoiled a magnificent view, so I had it torn down and the site seeded over to make a greensward.

Much of my inspiration has come from my travels, particularly to England and to Colonial Williamsburg, Virginia, where I like to spend every autumn to "recharge my batteries." Paula Dietz of *The New York Times* wrote that some of the planting schemes at Deerfield are "borrowed from Britain," and she likened certain areas, such as the Valley Garden, to parts of Windsor Great Park. While this is flattering, and I freely admit to "borrowing" ideas from many places, I prefer the challenge of trying to improve over the original and adapt it to Deerfield's unique surroundings. For example, having admired a distinctive, olive-colored, Colonial-style gate in the old English soldiers' graveyard (dating to 1690) at the rear of the gardens of the Governor's Palace at Colonial Williamsburg, I asked a local craftsman to produce a replica. However, I then painted it white to contrast better with Deerfield's lawn, and extended it on both sides with wide white rails to give it a more sleek appearance.

When Derek Fell and I discussed the need for this book, he felt it could help make a strong statement about "American" gardens. While the ethnic terms, "English", "Japanese", "French" and "Italian" do conjure up images of definite garden styles, it is very difficult to describe an "Amercian" garden, partly because of the vast range of climates in North America that prevent the development of a particular style, but also because of the varied landscape and the ethnic mix. I think this diversity is good, though it seems to have given rise to the notion abroad that American gardens are not very original and lag behind their counterparts in Europe. I do not agree. Though American gardens may draw on ideas from many cultures, the spectacular American landscape can stimulate some dramatically different gardens — witness the nearby duPont masterpieces near Wilmington, Delaware, and the great gardens of Charleston, South Carolina.

During the forty years of my life at Deerfield there never was a master plan. Fortunately, I didn't have to work with a tight budget or with a committee; I was able to make changes and improvements whenever I had the inspiration or the spirit moved me.

In landscaping Deerfield, I feel we pioneered new concepts in garden design in the creation of our Five Springs Garden. While clearing an overgrown thicket we discovered five freshwater springs bubbling up from the ground close to each other. We decided to highlight these by excavating deep channels to connect them, partially enclosing each spring with stone retaining walls. The individual flows combine to start a stream that feeds into Deerfield Pond, and the whole area is a labyrinth of meandering paths, stepping-stones and bridges. The resulting cool microclimate is ideal for moisture-loving plants, such as ferns, hostas, primulas and water iris. The Five Springs Garden is now a spectacular theme garden, the like of which I have seen nowhere else, either during my travels or in the course of my reading, and for some mysterious reason the birds enjoy it most of all.

Here at Deerfield we are fortunate to have verdant, rolling terrain with remnants of virgin woodland, natural flowing water and many mature specimens of native trees that seem to give the garden its special character. The landscape is very "English" in appearance, but with significant differences of detail: the soil is more acid, the winters more severe and the summers hotter and more humid. Dogwoods, azaleas and peonies grow more successfully here than anywhere in England and we capitalize on this advantage.

The seasons at Deerfield are extreme: winter can be very cold, with temperatures falling to -10°F; summer is very hot and humid, with temperatures rising to 90°F and more; spring is cool and green; autumn cool and golden. The average annual rainfall is forty-two inches. We have learned over the years which plants are "survivors," and there is always something beautiful to admire, even in the depths of winter, as Derek Fell's photographs demonstrate far better than my words. So please, sit back, relax and enjoy the show. More than anything I have ever done, creating this "American" garden has been (and still is) a lot of fun!

THE PHOTOGRAPHY

By Derek Fell

The photographs on pages 9, 61 and 88 were taken by Tom Hallowell, using Kodachrome 64 color transparency film. I photographed the rest, using Ektachrome 64 professional color transparency film. Tom uses a German *Leica* 35mm camera; I use a Japanese *Olympus* 35mm camera and also a German-made *Rollei* SLX, which shoots a larger-format slide or negative, size 2¼ x 2¼ inches. Both Tom and I have published books that explain in detail our individual photographic methods. *Life with a Leica* (Odyssey Productions) is a pictorial essay by Tom of his travels around the world shooting landscapes, people and wildlife. *How to Photograph Flowers, Plants & Landscapes* (HP Books) shows how I shoot pictures for publication.

Our individual preferences for different brands of camera and film in themselves prove an important point about photography — it's not so much the choice of camera that matters, but one's familiarity with the equipment. If you like a particular make of camera, stick with it; the same goes for film. You can make life too complicated by trying to contend with a lot of different cameras and films.

In photographing Deerfield, I looked for basically three kinds of composition: overall views, specific views and close-ups. The overall views help to establish a sense of place, give some idea of scope, capture a feeling of the environment; they generally produce the most stimulating pictures. In order to include enough of the surroundings, a wide-angle lens (28 mm) was sometimes used, but in the main a standard 50 mm lens worked well. Specific views usually concentrate on planting schemes and design concepts. They can show important features of a garden — a lake, a bridge, a border or waterfall, for example. Close-ups mostly highlight details of individual plants — a single flower, a cluster of berries, a group of leaves. You cannot create a good garden feature shooting only close-ups. They are mostly "fillers." It's the overall views — the vistas, in particular — that make readers gasp with admiration.

At Deerfield I preferred to shoot on overcast rather than sunny days. Because of the large amount of shade in the garden, and the inability of color film to capture detail in both brightly lit and dark shadow areas within the same exposure, an overcast day produces better pictures. It diffuses the light, reduces harsh contrasts and helps accentuate colors. During the height of the blooming period in spring, some of the best pictures of Deerfield were taken in light rain, which served to brighten up the colors even more than the diffused light alone.

I almost always used a tripod. This allowed me to keep the camera steady, thereby avoiding blurred images, and to shoot at slower shutter speeds so as to achieve the

Deerfield Pond in autumn, looking towards Rhododendron Hill shrouded in early morning mist.

maximum depth of field (area in sharp focus).

I chose Ektachrome 64 professional film because of its ability to render bright greens and clear blue skies — the two most important colors for landscape photography. It is available on special order from camera dealers. Kodachrome is generally superior for reds and yellows, but sometimes in poor light its greens can be too dark.

Tom likes to point out that luck plays a large part in getting good pictures, but he adds that one's chances of luck can be improved by hard work, and I support that notion. Whenever the slightest change in the weather suggested a different lighting situation I would rush twenty miles to Deerfield. Sometimes my luck was out — I left home one day in a beautiful snowstorm, believing that Deerfield would look fabulous, only to find that the fluffy snow had changed to heavy rain by the time I reached the garden. At other times, waiting an extra minute or turning that extra corner would produce a fantastic photographic opportunity.

Though floral displays seem to last for weeks, it is amazing how a garden changes from minute to minute when the light and mood become an important part of the composition. Wisps of mist and islands of light from a break in the clouds can be gone in a flash. Even a flowering crab apple and an azalea seem to have one particular day when they are each at their absolute peak of perfection. A day earlier or a day later can produce a totally different floral display.

Morning light always seems to yield the best pictures. After about 3.30 pm the setting sun casts a lot of reddish tones on film and, while this can be appealing for certain special effects, it is in my opinion unlikely to produce a pleasing picture, except, that is, for an actual sunset shot.

When everything else is technically correct — lighting, focus, exposure, shutter speed — the final criterion for a stunning picture is composition, and this you learn from practice and from looking at the work of good photographers. For me, a simple technique called "framing" works wonders. Instead of taking pictures of scenery as a flat panorama, consider adjusting your position so you have a clump of something in the foreground. It can be a spray of out-of-focus blossoms, some silhouetted leaves of a tree, lawn shadows on the ground — anything that helps fill in the edges like a picture frame.

"Backlighting" can enhance a garden scene. Instead of shooting with the sun always behind you, try some scenes with the sun ahead, particularly through trees. This will give translucent objects, such as leaves and flowers, a wonderful glow. However, you should use a lens hood to shade the lens from the sun or your exposures may show

Gate Garden at Deerfield. Mr. Hallowell found the original model for this gate in the Governor's Palace Garden, Colonial Williamsburg.

ugly streaks of extraneous light.

Except when photographing distant vistas, I hardly ever shoot at infinity. Needle-sharp pictures are better achieved by focusing on something definite in the middle ground, usually an interesting tree, a structure, or a clump of flowers.

One of the most exhilarating aspects of garden photography is seeing a breathtakingly beautiful scene, photographing it and, finally, seeing on film the scene as, or even better than you remembered it. This happens only rarely because the eye has a tendency to perceive images differently from the camera. But experience teaches one to recognize those occasions when the camera will enhance what registers with the naked eye. Deerfield has yielded more of those special images than any other garden I have ever photographed, not only because the garden is in an exquisitely beautiful setting, but also because Tom Hallowell's early interest in color photography was the main motivation behind the garden.

A HISTORY OF THE GARDEN

In 1946, H. Thomas Hallowell, Jr. and his wife, Dorothy, bought Deerfield, a thirty-five-acre farm with a fieldstone house, parts of it dating from 1804. They had been out driving one Sunday afternoon in December and saw the property with a "Sale" sign on it. By coincidence, the next morning, while cashing a check at his bank, Mr. Hallowell recognized Wayne Herknes, the real estate agent who had the property listed. Mr. Hallowell asked about the listing and Mr. Herknes replied: "Tom, that's my sister-in-law's place. It's just the house for you! When do you want to see it?" By 1.30 pm that same day, Mr. and Mrs. Hallowell were inspecting the property.

Mr. Herknes's brother had passed away several years before and, after living there alone since his death, his widow had decided to move to a smaller place. The fields had been abandoned and were choked with wild honeysuckle and poison ivy. A stream had been dammed to make a pond, but it was silted up with mud. Nevertheless, the property had a special atmosphere about it and the Hallowells thought it held exciting possibilities. There were no lawns, but a field in front of the house was flat and fertile, while at the back, the land sloped away steeply down to the stream creating a ravine, on the sides of which grew 200-year-old oaks and tall tulip poplars with trunks as straight as telephone poles.

An elderly farm hand, Tony, and his family lived in a shack that had an outhouse with a bathtub they filled from a hose. He had a summer helper who slept in a chicken coop. One of Mr. Hallowell's immediate concerns after purchasing the property was to keep Tony busy, and when a colorful mail-order catalog arrived featuring a long list of azalea varieties, he hit upon a solution. The new owner didn't know much about gardening at the time, but realized that if he planted a lot of small azaleas in long rows it would at least give Tony something to do. The smallest azaleas quoted in the catalog cost just five cents apiece, so 10,000 were ordered at a total cost of US$500. Mr. Hallowell chose at random by catalog description what sounded like a good selection of colors and kinds, with different flowering times. Truckloads of flats duly arrived, filled with the little plants, and with the help of an old horse that came with the property, Mr. Hallowell and Tony cultivated an acre of ground to accommodate them.

The azaleas grew phenomenally in their new home and, as time passed, to avoid overcrowding in the nursery, permanent places had to be found for them. Over the years the once barren fields were converted into luxuriant lawns, and then beds and borders were made for the azaleas. Some were replanted in island beds surrounded by lawn, others

Deerfield House and azalea hedge viewed from the front lawn in early spring. Portions of the house date to 1804.

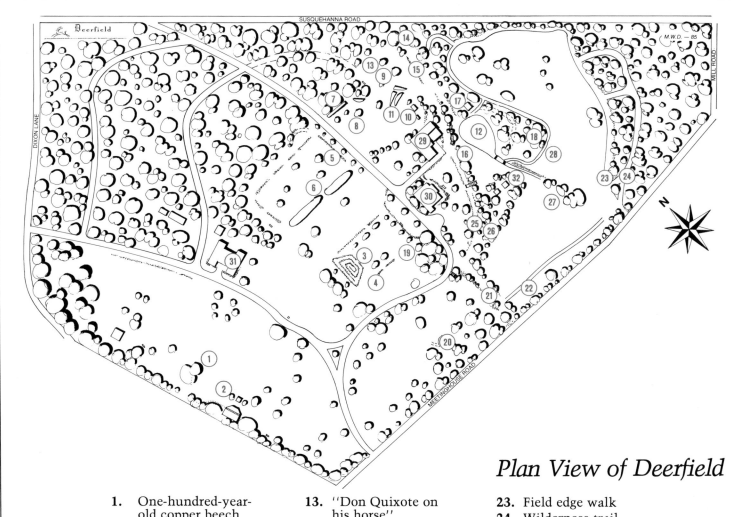

Plan View of Deerfield

1. One-hundred-year-old copper beech
2. Swimming Pool Garden
3. Maze
4. Rope swing
5. Williamsburg Gate and Garden
6. Peony beds
7. Perennial bed
8. Large Japanese cut-leaf maple
9. Sundial
10. Rose garden and corncrib
11. Cutting garden
12. Pond
13. "Don Quixote on his horse"
14. Boxwood allée (700 feet long)
15. Valley view bench
16. Springhouse and Pond view
17. Springhouse (1804)
18. Rhododendron Hill and "sulking bench"
19. Corner Fern Garden
20. Lower Fern Garden
21. Old Front Lane
22. Field path
23. Field edge walk
24. Wilderness trail and "Cathedral Vista"
25. Valley view boxwood walk
26. Old bathhouse walk
27. Five Springs Garden
28. Path to upper level
29. Barn and old stable yard
30. Residence
31. Caretaker's house and workshop
32. Old bathhouses and waterfalls

were arranged as undulating borders that followed the lines of the natural woodland at the edges of the property. In the rush to get the azaleas planted, every conceivable color combination was tried, resulting in a spontaneity of design and a pleasantly informal effect.

Shortly after the azaleas arrived, a bargain lot of 3,500 beautiful English boxwood plants was offered for sale by a local nursery. They were just six inches high and cost twenty cents each. Although he was undecided as to their eventual purpose, Mr. Hallowell bought the lot for US$700 and again Tony was kept occupied transplanting them into temporary nursery beds. As time went by, the boxwood plants were used to make hedges and avenues, some planted in straight lines to divide the garden into sections, others planted as curves to follow the contour of a slope or a winding path. The longest section is a 700-foot line of boxwood, more than half of it in double rows to make a leafy corridor.

In 1939 Mr. and Mrs. Hallowell had visited the maze at Hampton Court, England, and managed to get lost in it. A few years later they also visited the replica of the Hampton Court maze at the Governor's Palace in Colonial Williamsburg, where holly bushes form the hedges. Then, in about 1951, Mr. Hallowell saw a plan view of the Hampton Court maze in a magazine and suddenly had the idea of making a half-size duplicate of it on a new lawn in front of Deerfield House. The completed design contained more than 1,600 plants and used up half of the original boxwood he had growing in the nursery.

A few years after the Hallowells took possession of the estate, they wanted a name for their new property. Several were considered, but as Mr. Hallowell tells it, they had fields and the deer made a habit of visiting (they still do), so they put the fields and the deer together and named it "Deerfield."

Now, over forty years after the Hallowells moved in, Deerfield's fifty acres contain twenty-two acres of lawns, 7,000 azaleas, one hundred different kinds of trees and 4,500 feet of boxwood hedge. The maze is now four feet high and maintained at that height. Other impressive statistics include: 4,688 feet of paths wide enough to drive a golf cart along; 4,516 feet of paved roads; 348 steps; 248 stepping-stones; 2,588 feet of fencing; and 2,083 feet of stone walls.

The Hallowell family traces its roots back to John Hallowell, a Quaker farmer who emigrated from England in 1683, one year after William Penn landed at Philadelphia. His ship sailed up the Delaware River and landed not far from what is now Chester, south of Philadelphia. A few years later, he moved inland to a place called Hilltop, now known as Abington, the township where Deerfield is located.

Born in 1908, Mr. Hallowell scoffs at any suggestion that he inherited wealth: "What I inherited was an *opportunity*," he says. He became Plant Superintendent in his father's metalworking factory in 1932, Plant Manager during World War II, and eventually President. He is now Chairman of the Board of SPS Technologies Inc., which employs some 5,000 people in sixteen plants worldwide. The company today makes a wide variety of products: it is the world's largest supplier of precision aircraft engine parts and high-strength precision fasteners for airplanes. Of his sixty years' service with the company founded by his father Mr. Hallowell says: "I don't remember an unhappy day." Exuberant and full of good humor, he enjoys his life with Mrs. Hallowell to the full, expanding and improving the gardens at Deerfield and traveling widely. He is an emeritus trustee of Swarthmore College, Abington Memorial Hospital and the Franklin Institute. He is one of the overseers of the Wm. Penn Charter School and has been an industrial trustee of the Pennsylvania State University since 1950.

Mr. and Mrs. Hallowell have made substantial contributions to charity, particularly medical and educational institutions with which they have been associated over the years. Tom has been active in many local, state and national associations, his offices ranging from Vice President of the American Boxwood Society to President of the American Standards Association. "Life has been very busy," he says, "and Dorothy always did a great job of 'minding the store' while I was away."

"Whenever I've had a job to do I've always wanted to do it right and do it better," he says. The gardens began as a hobby, a diversion from his demanding workdays that offered little vacation time. "In my seventy-eighth year the garden is very important to me; as time goes on things seem to move faster, and I don't want to wait too long for results," he admits. "I have a fondness for bulldozers, cherry pickers, back hoes and golf carts — to get me around Deerfield in a hurry."

Today, Deerfield is a spectacular place to enjoy later years . . . to meditate and escape the pressures of a hectic world outside. But even now, almost every walk provokes new ideas for improvement — a new vista to open up, a slope to plant, a new bridge to build. It's a wonderful, peaceful, beautiful world, but more important to Mr. and Mrs. Hallowell, it is one that has produced a great deal of happiness.

Vista along the Old Front Lane, originally the front entrance to Deerfield. Spring blooms of azaleas and dogwoods color the edges of the lane.

Spring

The first sign of spring at Deerfield occurs towards the end of February, though snow may fall even until April 1. At the merest hint of warmer weather, purple-mottled spathes of skunk cabbage will thrust through the moist soil along the stream banks, closely followed by vivid green, cabbage-like leaves.

A more dramatic announcement of spring is soon made by the bright yellow forsythia and golden trumpet daffodils. Flowering at the same time as the forsythia — and in close proximity — is the delicate pink Korean rhododendron (*R. mucronulatum*), the two shrubs making a particularly attractive color combination.

Deerfield features a fine collection of pink and white saucer magnolias. Though the trees are hardy, the flowers appear well ahead of the leaves and are sensitive to frost. However brief the magnolia display may be, it is glorious. White and pink ornamental crab apples are next to steal the show, their billowing clouds of blossoms humming with bees.

By the first week of May the azaleas are in full bloom, with perhaps three quarters of the plantings in flower, coinciding precisely with the flowering impact of native dogwoods, both white and pink.

At this time of year the Hallowells love to invite friends on two open garden days to see the show, and Mr. Hallowell is up early each morning walking every corner of the property, checking to see if anything needs tidying up. He may also be seen riding around on a golf cart taking color pictures. "This time of year is so beautiful," he says, "it has the same effect on me as the first time I saw the Taj Mahal — it almost brings tears to my eyes."

Atop the Rhododendron Hill, in a clearing overlooking Deerfield Pond, is an English teak bench, one of fifteen scattered throughout the garden. Mr. Hallowell calls it his "sulking bench" because whenever he is in a poor mood (which is very seldom), he only has to sit on the bench and look out over the Valley Garden below for his spirits to be instantly raised!

Set into the side of the Rhododendron Hill is a stone-and-plaster springhouse dating to 1804. The ostrich ferns grow so luxuriantly here, among broad sweeps of pachysandra, that Mr. Hallowell calls it his "fern factory."

The spring extravaganza concludes with a mass flowering of herbaceous peonies and roses, some of the former with heads fully ten inches across, interplanted with foxgloves, lupines and columbine. There follows a brief lull as the garden seems to catch its breath before a profusion of annuals and summer-flowering bulbs continues the parade of color into the next season.

Above: *Trumpet daffodils blooming between clumps of still-dormant azaleas, in early spring.*

Right: *Clump of yellow forsythia and split-rail fence, along the Old Front Lane.*

Above left: *A study in tranquility: white flowering crab apple and an English teak bench make an inviting place to sit and admire the view on the upper lawn.*

Left: *Saucer magnolia blooms near the Gate Garden.*

Above: *Pink Korean rhododendron and yellow forsythia are perfect companions in a mixed shrub border.*

Pink flowering crab apple billowing over a border of azaleas just starting to show color.

Left: *The lower Valley Garden shaded by tall tulip poplar trees, looking downstream.*

Below: *Azalea-bordered steps leading from the lower Valley Garden up to the main house, in spring.*

19

Stone-and-plaster springhouse, built 1804 in the Valley Garden, surrounded by flowering azaleas.

20

View of the lower Valley Garden from the English teak bench fondly referred to by the owner as his "sulking bench" because of the ability of the view to raise his spirits.

Above left: *Spillway (foreground) and Rhododendron Hill (rear) shaded by tulip poplar trees.*

Middle left*: Climbing roses decorate a sheep hurdle used as a fence.*

Bottom left: *Family of Canada geese, who return every year to nest, swim across Deerfield Pond.*

Above: *View of Deerfield Pond and spillway from Rhododendron Hill.*

Above: *Upper Valley Garden with azalea-flanked steps leading up to the main house.*

Left: *Spectacular show of herbaceous peonies in one of the perennial borders.*

Summer

The most welcome sound during summer is that of falling rain. July and much of August can be hot and humid, with occasional thunderstorms, but it is not uncommon for Deerfield to go sixty days or more with very little rain.

In the Valley Garden, vast plantings of lilies — both *Lilium* and *Hemerocallis* — flower spectacularly in the dappled shade, while fragrant purple-and-white flower spikes of hosta arch out over large, paddle-shaped leaves.

Golden-yellow black-eyed Susans *(Rudbeckia hirta)* and vivid pink stonecrop *(Sedum spectabile)* are two outstanding perennials that cheerfully shrug off the heat and drought in the open flowerbeds, rubbing shoulders with vivacious blooms of tuberous dahlias.

Surrounding the old Swimming Pool Garden at the opposite end of the property, annual impatiens keep up a nonstop show in planters and beds bordering a water lily pool. Bright yellow marigolds, deep red zinnias, pink petunias and purple cosmos provide a continuous supply of cut flowers for the house, stimulated into an even greater frenzy of flowering every time they are cut.

A particularly successful summer planting scheme has been the naturalizing of hundreds of Mid-Century lilies along the shaded slopes of the lower Valley Garden. A thousand rhizomes were planted the first year as an experiment to see if they would thrive. Gorgeous flower spikes in red, pink, yellow, orange and white came up so thick along the high stream banks that Mr. Hallowell ordered a thousand more for autumn planting.

In a corner of one of the flower beds Mrs. Hallowell always reserves space for several tomato plants, held upright by wire "tomato towers." They are inspected almost daily to determine their progress, and the ripening of the first juicy red tomato fruits is heralded as a significant summertime event at Deerfield.

For the Hallowells, a favorite refuge from the heat is the lower Fern Garden, where paths of pine needles lead from one garden seat to another in the deep shade of tall evergreens. In the Valley Garden, too, shade and running water help create a cool microclimate and a pleasant escape from the baking heat of the lawns and meadows above.

But whatever the heat of midsummer suppresses, the cooler nights of late summer revive. Roses begin a second flush of bloom, lawns become verdant and bedding chrysanthemums form tightly-packed, russet-colored flower cushions that are a preview of the incredible colors of autumn to come.

Above: *Summer-flowering red water lily displays flawless beauty in a small formal pool near the Swimming Pool Garden.*

Right: *Large Japanese cut-leaf maple displays bronze leaf coloring in summer (compare this with its spectacular autumn coloring, page 69). Its delicate, feathery leaves make people want to reach out and stroke it like a shaggy dog.*

*One-hundred-year-old copper beech provides a cool, shady canopy on
a hot summer's day. Stepping-stone footpath leads visitors from one
side to the other, offering a close-up view of its massive grey trunk.*

Luxuriant bed of enormous ostrich ferns which multiply freely in the lower Valley Garden, below the spillway.

Line of native green ash trees decorates a meadow where gusts of wind make silvery waves among the tall grass.

Right: *Sedum "Autumn Joy" starts flowering in late summer, but the dried flower heads stay decorative through autumn and well into winter.*

Below: *Mixture of shade-loving hybrid lilies decorates the slopes of the lower Valley Garden, flowering prolifically in early summer, the orange flowers appearing slightly ahead of the red, pink and white.*

Left: *Handsome white pine framed by the silhouetted branches of other pines along a vista bordering the lower Fern Garden.*

Below: *Path of pine needles in the lower Fern Garden makes a pleasant place to walk during summer.*

Large decorative tuberous dahlia, variety ''Procyon'', has golden-yellow petals with fiery red tips — a stunning highlight in the summer flower garden.

Autumn

Around the middle of August there is a chill in the morning air. The slight temperature drop and the shortening day trigger a change in the leaves of deciduous trees. Sumac is the first to react, the lance-like leaflets turning shades of red, orange and purple. The Japanese maples are last and may not change color until November, when they become bright orange and molten-red.

Some of the leaf colors are as intense as any floral display. An early color change occurs with the burning bush *(Euonymus alatus)*. It is mostly seen elsewhere as a bushy shrub, but at Deerfield there is a magnificent tree specimen, the leaves of which turn brilliant red, accentuated by a dark background of evergreen pines.

Black tupelos *(Nyssa sylvatica)*, among the tallest trees at Deerfield, turn a red of similar intensity, and the wonder is they are not more widely grown in home gardens. The towering tulip poplars turn a golden yellow. After a shower on an overcast day, the normally grey trunks seem almost black and the contrast of the black bark with the golden leaves is dramatic.

Even after they have fallen, the leaves decorate the ground, providing a beautiful carpet to highlight the textures and colors of the tree trunks until they are finally swept up for the compost pile. Sometimes, in an Indian summer, leaves falling on the surface of the pond will cover it in an almost solid sheet of chestnut brown from end to end.

Beautiful red berries shine like rubies among the autumn leaves. A handsome Washington hawthorn tree near the back entrance generally produces an enchanting display, to the great delight of cardinals, chickadees and other songbirds which feast on the bitter fruits. One year the tree suffered serious damage from an ice storm that shattered its crown, but after Mr. Hallowell performed major surgery with a saw, it sprouted a new set of scaffold branches and soon regained its attractive shape.

Though the evergreens do not change color nor drop their leaves all at one time (but shed and replenish them continuously throughout the year), they are important components of the autumn and winter landscape. Not only are they good backgrounds against which to view the russet colors of the deciduous trees, they also give a sense of permanence and cohesiveness to the garden, whether they be pyramidal needle evergreens thrusting green spires to the sky, or broad-leaf evergreens, like boxwood and rhododendrons, with more compact, mounded outlines.

Even the most subtle color changes can be enchanting: many of the evergreen azaleas turn maroon and are exquisite after a hoarfrost has crystalized the leaf margins . . . a vivid reminder that winter is close at hand.

Above: *White gate and railings contrast beautifully with the russet colors of autumn, muted by early morning mist.*

Right: *Deerfield Pond in autumn, looking downstream, the mirror-smooth surface covered with fallen leaves.*

Above: *Broad grassy walk decked with fallen leaves sweeps along top of stream bank past a boxwood hedge towards Deerfield Pond.*

Left: *Black tupelo leaves show bright red autumn color at the edge of woodland.*

Old Front Lane in autumn colors, viewed from the main house (compare this with a similar view in spring, page 13).

Old springhouse framed by ostrich ferns in autumn colors, an incredible transformation from the colors of spring (page 20).

Above: *Grove of tulip poplars in the lower Valley Garden, seen from a trail on the opposite slope.*

Right: *Black tupelo trees in autumn finery, underplanted with evergreen azaleas.*

Above: *Fresh carpet of pine needles brightens the woodland floor in a grove of dark pines.*

Left: *Purple alyssum, edging a border of boxwood, flowers well during the cool days of autumn.*

Washington hawthorn in full-berried display. The bitter fruits provide food for songbirds.

Winter

Frost at Deerfield bites by November and light sprinklings of snow generally fall by Christmas, tinting the landscape as though it has been dusted with icing sugar. The ground freezes rock-hard by New Year's Day, and where it stays frozen the plants are secure, for they will remain dormant and viable. Where intermittent thawing and freezing occur, however, occasional winterkill can be a problem.

Some years snowfall is light, other years heavy: "friendly" snows transform Deerfield into a Christmas card scene; severe snows bring large snowflakes that sting your face as they fall. The latter are cold and heavy, causing branches to break and bushes to split apart.

The first priority after a snowfall is to brush the tops of the boxwood hedges. If the snow freezes on them it can cause ugly browning of leaves and heavy plant losses.

Around the drip-line of the house, special frames are placed over foundation evergreens to protect them from avalanches of snow cascading from the roof. Inside, on a chilly evening, the Hallowells like nothing better than watching television together in front of a log fire, with their dog between them on the sofa for company.

One of the most beautiful — yet potentially destructive — winter events is freezing rain. Falling gently in the night as light rain, it freezes on brittle branches. When the sun rises the garden is a wonderland of flashing sheaths of ice, twinkling like prisms at every contour in the advancing light. If the air stays still the dazzling spectacle is welcome and gone within hours, silently melted by the strengthening heat of the sun. But when a breeze springs up with the clearing skies, the air is filled with the sound of crashing boughs smashing their burdens of ice into smithereens. It is a frightening sound and the destruction can take weeks to clear up, and years for nature to repair.

Some trees and shrubs are naturally equipped to resist heavy accumulations of snow and ice, particularly the Atlas cedar *(Cedrus atlantica)*, native to the Atlas Mountains of North Africa. Its long, sweeping branches are like rubber, bending down to the ground without breakage. The evergreen azaleas also bear their mantles of snow with equanimity, each leaf supporting a little mound of fluffy snow like a cottonball.

Even bare of snow, the landscape is never without beauty. The leafless deciduous trees etch the skyline with an intricate tracery of branches. Mists linger in the low-lying areas and the world becomes filled with shrouded silhouettes . . . until that sunny, warm spell in February when the skunk cabbage blooms again and nature begins its cycle of miracles anew.

Above: *Hoarfrost on evergreen azalea leaves is a sure sign of approaching winter.*

Right: *Deerfield Pond in winter, looking downstream (compare this with the front cover showing a similar scene in spring).*

Springhouse set into the side of Rhododendron Hill, surrounded by snow (check pages 20 and 37 for the same scene in spring and autumn).

English teak bench on Rhododendron Hill offers a serene view of the lower Valley Garden covered in snow.

Above: *View looking upstream from the extremity of the lower Valley Garden after a heavy snowfall. Rocky stream quickens its flow under an arched wooden footbridge.*

Right: *"Skyline trees" are an important feature of the winter landscape. Here, tulip poplar and beech tower over an underplanting of evergreen rhododendrons to frame a distant grove of pines.*

Opposite: *View of upper Valley Garden, looking upstream from the springhouse.*

Left: *Old Front Lane wearing a mantle of snow, seen from the main house (for the same view in spring and autumn, see pages 13 and 36).*

Below: *Azalea bushes appear to be covered in cottonballs after a coating of fresh snow.*

Above: *Wooden bridge and forty-nine stone steps dusted with a light sprinkling of snow in early winter.*

Right: *Mixed border of trees and shrubs seems frosted with icing sugar after a light fall of snow.*

Above: *Atlas cedar draped in heavy snow. Rubbery branches allow this attractive conifer to carry heavy burdens of snow without breakage.*

Left: *A "white-out" at Deerfield. Split-rail fence marks boundary between natural woodland of the Valley Garden and an open meadow. Buildings in background on far side of slope are old stables.*

The Azaleas

Deerfield's azaleas bloom over a three-month period starting in early March. They are not fertilized, since the soil at Deerfield is naturally acid and azaleas are extremely efficient at extracting all their nutrient needs from the layers of mulch applied to the beds every year in the form of shredded pine bark.

Though the deciduous azaleas are treated like rhododendrons and left largely unpruned, the evergreen azaleas are sheared with electric hedge-trimmers after blooming. Flowers for the next season are produced on new growth and the shearing can be done up to September 1 without affecting the next season's floral display. Evergreen kinds represent more than ninety per cent of the azalea plantings, in white and shades of pink, purple and red. The few deciduous azaleas are mostly yellow and orange and are highly fragrant.

Azaleas and rhododendrons belong to the same botanical family, *Rhododendron*, but the azaleas, though smaller-leaved and smaller-flowered, make a much bigger splash of color, with blossoms sometimes so numerous they will completely hide the foliage. In places, three distinct colors of azalea have been planted so close together they have merged with each other to form what appears to be a single multicolored shrub — white, red and pink flowers creating a solid mound of vibrant color.

Three large beds of azaleas in front of Deerfield House came about by accident. Originally, Mr. Hallowell had three apple trees there, purchased from a Sears, Roebuck catalog, and to make them more ornamental he ringed them with different colors of azaleas. Like most orchard trees, however, the apples were difficult to keep healthy and eventually they had to be removed, leaving the azaleas to take over each site completely.

In another unusual azalea planting, two parallel hedges have been cut square to form solid "balustrades" edging steps leading up to the house from the Valley Garden. It doesn't seem possible that an evergreen azalea planting could be so severely pruned and yet flower so spectacularly, but at Deerfield all things are possible.

Even out of bloom, the evergreen azaleas are highly ornamental. Throughout the summer their mounded forms give substance and shape to shrub borders; in autumn the leaves of many change color to shades of maroon and wine-red. When winter arrives, the azaleas are especially attractive after frost, with the margins of each leaf outlined in ice crystals. After a snowfall, every bush looks like a flowering cotton plant, each leaf supporting a dollop of snow.

Above: *Kurume azalea blossoms with fresh spring foliage sprouting through the dense mass of shimmering rose-pink flowers.*

Right: *Beds and borders crowded with azaleas at the edge of woodland. This is a fascinating area to explore by golf cart.*

Steps leading from the Valley Garden to the main house, cut through a gap in the boxwood allée. Sides of stairway are edged in azaleas, sheared to a "squared" shape.

Tall trunks and arching branches of black tupelo trees and tulip poplars create high shade perfect for an underplanting of azaleas.

Left: *Evergreen hybrid azalea makes a perfect dome of brick-red flowers in spring.*

Below: *Orange-flowering deciduous azalea contrasts brilliantly with rosy-red blossoms of an evergreen rhododendron.*

56

Right: *Three distinct colors of azalea — red, pink and white — merge so perfectly, they seem to be a single plant.*

Below: *A blizzard of flowers in spring! These "Delaware Valley White" azaleas appear to be mounds of snow.*

Above: *Azaleas and rhododendrons make a winning combination in a mixed shrub border.*

Right: *Azalea "Viola" beside the stream in the lower Valley Garden. White and pink flowering dogwoods color the high slope beyond.*

58

Deerfield Maze

A half-size replica of the yew maze at Hampton Court, England, which dates from circa 1700, Deerfield Maze contains 1,600 plants of English boxwood *(Buxus sempervirens)*. It receives no special care except for an annual trimming before new growth begins in spring. About half the new growth of the previous year is cut back with electric hedge-shears, the whole process taking thirty-two hours.

The Hampton Court maze is a third of an acre in size, with half a mile of walkways. Though "turf" mazes involving patterns on the ground date back to Medieval times, the Hampton Court maze is believed to be the world's first "hedge" maze. Laid out in the reign of King William III, when he resided at Hampton Court, the construction is credited to two of his gardeners, named London and Wise.

Maze-trimming is an art that Mr. Hallowell mastered many years ago. "It is not an occupation that attracts many new practitioners and today there aren't many of us long-time maze-trimmers left," he explains. "It requires a special talent since you don't put up strings to guide your cutting; rather, you have to do the job by feel." In recent years he has passed on the art to groundskeeper, Bob Hill.

The maze is maintained at about forty-eight inches since it is aesthetically most pleasing at just that height; even so, it has taken almost forty years to get there because of boxwood's naturally slow growth. Faster-growing yew, hemlock, beech and holly are much more popular choices for mazes, but they lack the dense foliage cover of English boxwood and their lines are never as clean or sharp.

Children can wander the narrow, leafy passages of the Deerfield Maze and enjoy the excitement of getting thoroughly lost, while adults can peer over its hedges and find the middle with little hesitation; short people are advised to imitate Theseus, of Greek mythology, and leave a trail of string in order to find their way out again.

The site of the maze at Deerfield has proven so suitable that no fertilizing or watering has been necessary, only mulching each year with shredded pine bark. Still, the making of a maze, one of the most challenging of all horticultural endeavors, is not to be taken lightly; and in this case its success is a tribute to good gardening, patience and the owner's good humor.

Deerfield Maze is a half-size replica of the Tudor-style maze at Hampton Court, England (opposite view from that shown on the back cover).

Wide-angle lens, shooting from a cherry picker fifty feet above the ground, allows the entire design of Deerfield Maze to be seen.

Superiority of English boxwood over other hedging material is evident in this overhead view, showing dense, green growth and clean, sharp lines.

63

Above: *Deerfield Maze from overhead in early autumn, when yellow tulip poplar leaves start to fall from branches overhanging the area.*

Right: *Deerfield Maze in winter, covered in snow. Brooms are used to sweep away the heavy coating before it has a chance to freeze and cause damage.*

The Trees

Trees have a habit of becoming the most dominant life forms in a landscape and Deerfield is no exception. Recognizing the power of trees to establish a strong sense of beauty and grandeur, Mr. Hallowell has made special efforts to preserve those indigenous to the property and also to acquire splendid specimens originating elsewhere.

A particular favorite is a one-hundred-year-old copper beech. It has a five-foot diameter trunk, a 375-foot circumference and a perfect dome shape, with branches that sweep to the ground. One day, seeking shelter during a rain shower, Mr. Hallowell stepped inside the leafy canopy and all at once, after many years of passing by the tree, he noticed the beauty of the gnarled grey trunk, resembling an elephant's hide. A stepping-stone walk was promptly constructed from one side to the other under the tree's spreading branches and rustic seats were placed at strategic points so the massive old trunk can be admired at leisure. A carpet of golden-brown pine needles not only makes walking over the protruding tree roots more comfortable, it also provides a perfect natural contrast to the ancient grey trunk and the dark purple leaf canopy.

When five great 200-year-old oaks began to fall victim to gypsy moth attacks, Mr. Hallowell was despondent. But, as he says: "It's an ill wind that doesn't blow some good," and in fact the loss of the trees let in more light to an under-story planting of rhododendrons and azaleas, which grew and flowered better once the oaks were gone.

Several especially beautiful younger trees are a graceful clump of paper birch, a large Japanese cut-leaf maple and a spectacular weeping form of Norway spruce. The birch clump came from a local nursery that was going out of business, but about ten years after it was planted a sleet and ice storm severely damaged the top. Mr. Hallowell pruned it drastically and after a few years its original graceful shape was restored. The cluster of elegant white trunks contrasts beautifully with the dark expanse of surrounding lawn, and in autumn its leaves turn buttercup-yellow.

A more costly proposition involved the large Japanese cut-leaf maple estimated to be over a hundred years old. Mr. Hallowell received a call from a local resident who was retiring to Florida and wanted a good home for it. The magnificent tree grew on his front lawn, its dense, feathery foliage draped all the way to the ground and even sweeping sideways across the lawn. "It was standing there just like a pretty girl," says Mr. Hallowell, and he soon had it moved the twenty miles to Deerfield. "There was no guarantee it would survive, but while we were excavating a hole for the 6,000-pound, eight-foot-diameter root ball, we found an old rusty horseshoe about eighteen inches down. Then I

Above: *Japanese cut-leaf maple showing purple spring foliage. In autumn the leaves undergo an incredible color change (see page 69).*

Right: *Pink and white dogwoods backlighted by the morning sun, viewed from the upper Valley Garden.*

remembered an old saying that if you bury a horseshoe with a tree, the tree will live, so I personally put it in the center of the hole.'' Now in its third year of residence at Deerfield, the tree is as attractive as ever and treated like a member of the family.

Soon after this purchase, Mr. Hallowell was looking at a collection of conifers in a nursery and spotted a weeping Norway spruce that looked remarkably like a horse and rider. ''I got so excited, I pointed it out to the owner, who hadn't previously seen the resemblance; just then I know the price went up twenty per cent,'' he says ruefully.

Regardless, the animated horse and rider now command a prominent place in the Sundial Garden, and the tree is affectionately nicknamed ''Don Quixote'' for the Spanish nobleman and his horse which it seems to imitate.

Top Left: *Weeping Norway spruce is affectionately known as "Don Quixote" because of its striking resemblance to a horse and rider.*

Bottom Left: *Burning bush tree in winter (compare this with spring and autumn appearances, pages 70 and 71).*

Above: *Large Japanese cut-leaf maple turns from purple to molten-red in autumn.*

Burning bush (Euonymus alatus), *grown into a tree, has bright green foliage in spring.*

Same trees as facing page, in full autumn coloring (for a winter look, see page 68).

Left: *Panorama of evergreen and deciduous trees flanking Deerfield Pond. Wooden structures are old bathhouses that once overlooked a swimming pool.*

Above: *Dogwoods and azalea blossoms light up an area of natural woodland.*

Left: *One-hundred-year-old copper beech has a 375-foot circumference and a five-foot trunk diameter.*

Above: *The silvery-white trunks of a clump of paper birch (Betula papyrifera) contrast with the mint-green lawn.*

The Vistas

The owner of a large English estate once said: "A view is worth a thousand blooms; a lake is worth ten thousand." Mr. Hallowell agrees wholeheartedly with that opinion.

One of the most impressive vistas at Deerfield is the Old Front Lane, which was the original driveway to the house. After Mr. Hallowell purchased the additional acreage, he decided to use the main entrance of the new property, and then was faced with the problem of what to do with the old driveway. He took up the blacktop surface and lined it with beautiful native dogwoods, their shimmering pink-and-white blossoms in spring rising into the overhead foliage canopy like flocks of butterflies. Some tall ash trees arch completely over the old lane, creating a tunnel of high shade ideal for azaleas. So, the edges of the lane were planted with azaleas that had outgrown their original locations, and the driveway itself was grassed over, completing a beautiful vista similar to the *allées*, or avenues, popular in French châteaux gardens.

In order to enhance a distant feature and establish an uninterrupted view, a great deal of "lower branch pruning" is practiced at Deerfield. This generally involves cutting off lower limbs, leaving a high, pencil-straight trunk that encourages a shapelier crown.

Boxwood is used to direct the eye along many of the vistas. One particular boxwood corridor begins as a gently-curving walk below the house. It then dips and climbs and straightens out to form a single hedge, delineating a vista that is overhung by tall trees. There is a tingle of excitement at the beginning of the walk since it evokes an air of mystery — rather like a ghost tunnel — and offers surprises along its entire 700-foot length. At intervals the boxwood opens up to reveal a bench from which to admire a panoramic view of the Valley Garden, or a flight of slate steps descending to the pond.

The newest, and in many ways the most surprising vista, was recently opened up as a result of making trails through several acres of rough woodland inhabited by families of deer, foxes and raccoons. At one point the trail emerges from the dark woodland onto a sunlit meadow to reveal a beautiful far view of Deerfield House spotlighted in a clearing on the wooded slope opposite. The best way to appreciate this vista is from within the rough woodland before the trail emerges into the sunlight. A grove of towering pines forms huge columns, framing the distant house like the doorway of a Gothic cathedral.

Above: *Grove of tulip poplars on Rhododendron Hill viewed from the back door of Deerfield House.*

Right: *"Cathedral Vista." Trunks of large white pines form columns like those of a Gothic cathedral to frame Deerfield House on distant slope across open meadow.*

View from front door of Deerfield House in spring. A section of the maze can be seen at right of the white azaleas.

Vista across Valley Garden from the living room windows at rear of Deerfield House.

Left: *Vista looking downstream from a pair of old bathhouses in the upper Valley Garden.*

Above: *Boxwood vista, leading from the main house to the lower Valley Garden, in autumn.*

81

Left: *Mirror-like reflection on Deerfield Pond after a light, early-morning sprinkling of snow.*

Below: *A study in evergreens — English ivy on the barn wall, pines on the lawn, azaleas and boxwood on the slope — all in different shades of green, lightly tinted with fine snow. Corncrib is a relic of the old farmstead.*

The Boxwood

English boxwood *(Buxus sempervirens)* is one of the most versatile plants in cultivation. Despite its rather low profile as a lone plant, it undergoes a stunning transformation when used in a mass, at the hands of a good garden-maker.

The Latin *sempervirens* means "everlasting." In some of the great gardens of Italy there are boxwood hedges that are 300 years old yet just three feet high, kept low and compact by rigorous pruning. One of English boxwood's virtues is its excruciatingly slow rate of growth — about one inch a year.

Boxwood is native to lands around the Mediterranean: in Italy and Greece it is possible to enter an ancient boxwood forest where the plants have grown tree-like, to thirty feet in height, with gnarled, twisted, sinuous trunks and such a dense foliage cover, the forest floor is in perpetual darkness. Such forests are all the more eerie on a misty morning when the trees appear almost supernatural and the pleasant, peppery odor of the leaves pervades the air.

The wood of boxwood is rock-hard and valued for carving. The plants are reasonably hardy, evergreen and tolerate both alkaline and acid soils. The leaves are small, oval, smooth and glossy green, the flowers greenish, inconspicuous, rarely noticed. No wonder some people think of boxwood as a plant that just sits there and does nothing.

Left alone, boxwood forms a billowing, rounded shape and this was the favorite way of growing it in the old plantation gardens of Virginia and elsewhere in the south. There, centuries-old plantings form thick, impenetrable hedges for screens and windbreaks, as well as passageways giving access from one section of a garden to another. More than any other plant, boxwood can establish a strong sense of design and structure in a garden, whether the desired effect be informal or formal.

Boxwood withstands heavy pruning to make formal shapes like a maze, or whimsical figures as in topiary work. It can be "squared" to make a clean, sharp edging for beds and borders, or it can be shaped as "meat balls" to soften the edges of a path like cushions of moss.

Here's an interesting little exercise: study the accompanying pictures of boxwood at Deerfield (also the Maze, pages 60 to 65, and Boxwood Vistas, pages 81 and 88) and decide which of the following opinions you agree with:

"There is an American Boxwood Society that 'Boxophiles' should consider joining if all other societies are full."

Michael A. Dirr

"The beauty of boxwood *(Buxus sempervirens)* hardly needs to be pointed out."

Henry Mitchell

Above: *Boxwood allée in autumn — part of a continuous planting that extends some 700 feet.*

Right: *Boxwood hedge edges a slope intensively planted with azaleas, giving form and structure to this colorful section of the lower Valley Garden.*

The Lawns

There are more than twenty-two acres of lawns and grass paths at Deerfield. Bob Hill, head groundskeeper, took a two-year course in turf management at Penn State University and was assistant groundskeeper on a local golf course before coming to the estate, where he directs a staff of four. The lawns are his special pride.

Lawn maintenance today includes seeding bare spots that occur mostly as a result of drought and crows seeking grubs in the turf. When an area needs reseeding, a special seed mixture is made up, appropriate to the site. "Pennfine" perennial ryegrass is used predominantly in full sun, while fescues are added for planting in shade. White muslin is laid over newly-seeded areas to hold the seed down and prevent moisture loss. It is taken up once the grass is established and can be reused several times.

The lawns are fed twice a year — in spring, just as new growth begins, and again in autumn to help the grass establish a strong root system. "Fall feeding is the most important," notes Bob Hill, "if you only have time to feed once, do it then."

At one time the lawns and paths at Deerfield were seeded almost exclusively with Kentucky bluegrass varieties, but after a severe drought in 1980 killed off every blade of bluegrass, a switch was made to "Pennfine" improved perennial ryegrass, an introduction from Penn State University. "The old varieties would not cut clean," says Bob Hill, "rather, they had a tendency to shred and bleach at the ends. The new ryegrasses cut clean, are less prone to drought and disease, and are indistinguishable from bluegrass."

For most situations Bob Hill uses a mix that includes fifty per cent improved perennial ryegrass, forty per cent bluegrass and ten per cent red fescue. In addition to "Pennfine", five other improved ryegrasses are blended into every mix. The most favored bluegrass is "Pennstar", though four other varieties are included to make a well-integrated stand with maximum resistance to moisture stress and diseases. In shady locations, a heavier proportion of fescue is used, usually "Pennlawn" creeping red fescue.

One of the most effective uses of grass is on a path. Though it generally requires constant "patching" to keep it lush, nothing is quite as comfortable on the feet or as restful to the eye.

The lawns are particularly beautiful in the early morning and in the late afternoon when the sun is low in the sky and the surrounding trees cast long shadows across the velvet greensward. "I don't know if anyone has ever done a study of lawn patterns in garden design, but I know that they are important," says Mr. Hallowell.

Picture-perfect lawn blends improved perennial ryegrasses with bluegrasses for attractive looks and good drought resistance.

Shadows cast by morning sun pattern an expanse of lawn bordered by azaleas and dogwoods.

Broad grassy path invites exploration of a secluded area of Deerfield. The path sweeps down from the main house between plantings of azaleas and boxwoods, turning towards a shaded lawn in the upper Valley Garden.

Parting Shots

After this book was put together and the picture selections made for each season and each section, there still remained many beautiful images begging to be included. Ruthlessly, they were thinned out, leaving just six to take readers "once more around the block."

Left: Roseum Elegans, an outstanding Ironclad hybrid rhododendron, by the back entrance. Though azaleas are the scene-stealers in spring, their bigger cousins, the rhododendrons, try hard to outdo them. Other eye-catching varieties include "Windbeam," a Nearing hybrid that almost smothers itself in small, rounded, pale-pink flower trusses, and "Wissahickon," a shimmering-red Gable hybrid.

Right: The upper Valley Garden, looking from the Five Springs Garden towards Deerfield Pond. The Valley Garden is almost an eighth of a mile long, landscaped along its entire length. Bubbling up from springs in the ground, a stream cascades over two waterfalls, then flows along a flume into the pond. At the far end of the pond the water drops over a spillway, then meanders through a steeply-wooded ravine and under a wooden footbridge, finally leaving the garden beneath a fieldstone road bridge to feed into nearby Pennypack Creek, a tributary of the Delaware River.

Next page: A wooded slope overlooking the pond is underplanted with rhododendrons and threaded with footpaths which in autumn are covered with fallen leaves, the crisp, parchment-brown leaf litter in rich contrast with the large, leathery, evergreen rhododendron leaves and pachysandra ground cover.

Page 93: From a clearing on the Rhododendron Hill, there is a magnificent view of the house sitting snug on the crest of the opposite slope, with a light showing in Mr. Hallowell's office. When a covering of snow suffocates the land, to set footprints on any part of it seems a desecration.

Charming smaller tableaux are found in unexpected places . . . an old millstone gathering a garland of ivy as it rests in the stable yard awaiting a place in the garden beyond the plaster wall . . . stepping-stones leading along a primrose path to a stone seat in a sunken garden that was once a swimming pool . . . a rope swing suspended from a tall tulip poplar . . . and other pleasant surprises. But however perfect Deerfield may seem, it is still a garden in the making, undergoing constant improvement at the hands of a man who only ever wants to do things right and "make things better." Also, there is always the hand of nature making every season a different visual experience in this truly unique "American" garden.

Above: *Rhododendron* Roseum Elegans *by the back entrance.*

Opposite: *Lower Valley Garden in spring, with primroses flowering among rockery in the foreground.*

Fallen leaves carpet a narrow footpath running along a spillway towards Rhododendron Hill. Dense cover of evergreen pachysandra grows over the lower slope.

Snow-clad slope seen from Rhododendron Hill, looking up towards the main house. Lighted window is Mr. Hallowell's office.

CONCLUSION

By Jane G. Pepper, President, Pennsylvania Horticultural Society

When Derek Fell featured Deerfield Garden in the Society's magazine, *The Green Scene*, I think many people were thrilled to discover that such a magnificent garden existed in North America, let alone the Delaware Valley.

Mr. Hallowell is an active member of the Society and has kindly opened his garden to members during the azalea season. His accomplishments in business and community affairs are well known, and now I am happy to see similar recognition for his skill in landscape design for, make no mistake about it, though he uses accomplished landscape contractors and tree services to carry out planting, maintenance and construction work, the ideas are *his*.

What is more, I think Mr. Hallowell represents a type of horticultural spirit long alive in Europe and the Orient, that is now making a reputation for "American" garden design.

Thank you, Tom Hallowell, for making such a beautiful garden . . . and Dorothy Hallowell, whose partnership gave you the freedom to do it. Thank you, also, for such a sumptuous book that allows the world to share its wonders.

Old millstone in stable yard covered with English ivy.

Primrose path in sunken garden that was once a swimming pool.

INDEX